FROM FREEMASONRY TO FREEDOM

FROM FREEMASONRY TO FREEDOM

Stanley Trickett

Terra Nova Publications

First published by Terra Nova Publications Ltd, 1999
All rights reserved.

© *Stanley Trickett, 1999*

Stanley Trickett asserts the moral right
to be identified as the author of this work
[except 'suggestions for prayer']

Suggestions for prayer © *Terra Nova Publications Ltd, 1999*
All rights reserved.

Published in Great Britain by
Terra Nova Publications Ltd
PO Box 2400
Bradford on Avon, Wiltshire BA15 2YN

Unless otherwise stated, Scripture quotations are
taken from the Holy Bible, New International Version,
© *1973, 1978, 1984 by the International Bible Society.*
Used by permission of Hodder and Stoughton Ltd.
All rights reserved.

ISBN 1 901949 05 2

Cover design: Gazelle Creative Productions
Cover printed by The Shires Press, Trowbridge, Wiltshire

Printed in Great Britain at
The Cromwell Press, Trowbridge, Wiltshire

Contents

Preface

The purpose of this book is to bear witness to the love of God in Jesus Christ. This love is real, and it is made known through the Holy Spirit, who always glorifies Jesus.

To be of any use or help to others, a testimony must be honest about the difficulties as well as the wonderful blessings in life. My pilgrimage has been difficult at times, and as a Christian minister I know that this is true for many Christians. So I have been frank about the challenges I have faced.

But, throughout my life, I have experienced the bountiful grace of God, and it is to make known His wonderful love which is always there, even in the midst of life's problems, that I have written this book. His love is always sufficient to sustain and uphold those who come to Him. We come first to the Cross, in repentance. The price for sin was paid by Jesus, and we need to accept him personally as Lord and Saviour. Then we need to be open to the empowering of the Holy Spirit and the precious teaching of the written Word of God, the Bible. When I was first called to the ordained ministry, I knew that God was real, yet I did not know Him personally. I did not know the power of the Word;

nor had I experienced the real power and baptism of the Holy Spirit. These good things were yet to come. In this book I set out, quite simply, the things I experienced.

Why the title 'From Freemasonry to Freedom'? There are many things which can be barriers to our knowing God and experiencing His best for us. For me, the major barrier was an allegiance and vows which had to be repudiated before God could have His way in my life. This was the turning point, after which I was conscious of God's wonderful grace and blessings in a completely new way. For me, that had been the barrier.

Of course there are many other kinds of barrier, such as doubt, fear, unbelief, and all the other kinds of disobedience to the Word of God, of which people who desire to know God must repent and be freed. In my own experience, freemasonry had involved making terrible vows, and it failed to acknowledge Jesus Christ as the unique Son of God—divine as well as human; the only Mediator; the only One whose death can avail for sin: the Way, the Truth and the Life. The vows we make with our lips do very much matter to God. (See Matthew 12:37). It also matters very much indeed for our eternal salvation that we believe in our hearts God raised Jesus from the dead, and that we confess with our lips that Jesus is Lord. (See Romans 10:10). These are not optional extras—they are Christian basics, and if things we have said or done, or vows and allegiances we have taken on, run counter to these truths, then we need to be released. This can be done by repentance, and a spiritual 'cutting-off' from the things that are keeping us from that closeness to God which He wills for us. I describe how this happened for me. In case your need is similar to mine, I offer some suggestions for prayer at the end of this book. Having made a personal commitment to Jesus Christ, there is no substitute for belonging to a Christian church, where the Bible is believed and faithfully taught, where there is openness to the work of the Holy Spirit, and where you can enjoy both wise pastoring and fellowship with others who are seeking to grow in obedience to the Lord and proclaim the Gospel to a needy world.

Of course, when we experience hard things in life, it hurts. We live in a fallen world, and the effects of the sins and disobedience of fallen mankind are all around us. But in the midst of even the hardest circumstances, we can know the upholding love and kindness of the heavenly Father. Every difficulty provides fresh opportunity to grow in love and faithfulness. All good things come from God. All evil things come from the disobedience of man or the malevolence of Satan. We declare that 'all things work together for good, for those who love God.'

I have included a letter from my wife, written after the diagnosis of her Alzheimer's Disease, both because that letter has helped others, and because it bears witness that *nothing at all* can separate a Christian from the love of God.

Jesus did not promise his followers that life would always be easy! But he did promise that, "...I am with you always, to the very end of the age" (Matt.28:20b). What a tremendous encouragement to persevere. It is, like all the promises of Jesus, absolutely trustworthy. In the last analysis, everything else in life ceases. Worldly wealth and status will count for nothing when we come to meet Christ, as we surely shall in the world to come. Those who take Jesus at his word will not be disappointed.

Chapter One

GROWING UP

I remember my childhood as a very happy one. I was next to youngest of six children. For our parents, the family was their pride and joy. My father was the son of a wealthy farmer but, because he objected to his own father's second marriage, he had been turned out of his home without a penny, and forced to work for a pittance as a farm labourer. The bitterness which he felt about this did, in fact, stay with him for the rest of his life—but so, also, did a determination that none of his children would suffer as a result. They were to have only the best. And we did!

Money was very short, yet as children we always had a comic and some sweets at the weekend, when father had been paid. And this was indicative of the love which was lavished upon us by our parents throughout our childhood. Our home was indeed a happy home, and I have clear memories of long walks together, summer picnics, games in the garden, singing around the piano, (my father was an accomplished pianist) and the welcoming of visitors to tea on a Sunday.

One Sunday when there were no visitors, I remember rashly saying to my mother, who had just produced a freshly-baked cake from the oven, "Oh—lovely—I could eat *all* of that myself...." Instead of rebuking me for being so greedy, she said quietly, "Alright—here you are," and then began cutting slice after slice, putting it on my plate. After the third slice I began to feel embarrassed, for I knew I could not eat any more! She had wisely taught me a lesson in her own way—but it was a lesson I never forgot.

We lived some two miles from the village church and, although our parents rarely went to church, they certainly encouraged us to go. We thought nothing of walking the two miles each way on a Sunday morning— and sometimes again on a Sunday evening. The services must have been dreadfully dull, yet we never missed going, nor did it ever occur to us that we might not go. I must say I was never conscious of meeting God, either in church or elsewhere, yet somehow the saying of prayers night and morning became very important to me. Indeed, I went through one phase in which I believed that unless I prayed for *everyone, every night*, God would not look after them! So my prayer-time became longer and longer. I was really quite afraid of leaving anyone out! Despite all this, I never felt that God was close, nor that He was answering any of my specific prayers—but, nevertheless, I was too afraid either to miss out my prayers or even to shorten them. I was not quite sure what God would do to me—or to them—if I did!

We all attended the village school, and were greatly

encouraged by our parents to succeed in exams, and so pave the way to a good higher education. But that was not to be, and we could hardly blame them for being so disappointed in us as we failed exam after exam.

For me, there was no alternative but to leave school at the age of fourteen and seek employment. Four years in the local post office were followed by two and half years of national service in the Royal Air Force, most of which was spent in Egypt. It was here that I met God for the first time. This encounter took place during the beautiful service of Compline, which was led by a very loving and godly padre in the camp chapel. The sheer peace and Presence at this service almost overwhelmed me, and I remember thinking, "So *this* is what it is like to meet with God. I want this feeling to stay with me always."

It did not, of course—but that was my fault, not God's. It was here I recognised that, through the excellent educational facilities offered by the RAF, I could retake the exams I had failed—and more. Which is what I did; this time with very different results—and very proud parents.

Whilst working in the post office, I met the girl of my dreams, Kathleen, with whom I shared a love of dancing, tennis, music and Shakespeare. Most important of all, she was a practising Christian, who loved her Church, and for whom Sunday worship was always a high priority. She was a girl of great integrity and high moral standards, and we spent many hours talking about the Christian way of life and how difficult it was to maintain. Yet we both knew that this must be our aim—nothing less. We corresponded regularly throughout my national service and, a few months after my return, I proposed to her. It was while we were out on one of our favourite walks on Haughmand Hill. We had stopped for a rest and had been sharing some verses from A.E. Housman's *Shropshire Lad*, when the moment seemed right! We made plans to get married in Shrewsbury, in the beautiful church of St. Chad.

Chapter Two

FOR BETTER OR WORSE

How well I remember that day! My national service had taught me the importance of punctuality and careful planning, so our wedding had been organised with military precision! The service was due to start at 12.00 noon. At 11.55 a.m. the organist would play through one of our favourite pieces of music, *Jesu, Joy of Man's Desiring* and, as it was played through a second time, the bride would arrive at the chancel step. What we had not taken into account was the volume of traffic in the locality on a Saturday morning, so it was not until 12.15, with the organist playing our chosen piece through for the umpteenth time, and the congregation knowing every note by heart, that the bride arrived!

But the wedding day was memorable for another reason. I had thought that I knew my wife fairly well, but the sincerity with which she took those marriage vows amazed even me, coupled as they were with a complete and utter offering to God of our marriage and the rest of our lives, come what may. Little did we know how our lives together would develop, or what the future would hold.

My career in the Civil Service had been progressing favourably, but having now acquired additional educational qualifications, my thoughts turned towards the possibility of a career in teaching. I needed references, so who better to approach than my parish priest? It was then that the bombshell dropped. After listening quietly for a few moments, the vicar, without even mentioning my request for a teaching reference, looked me straight in the eye, saying, "Have you ever considered ordination?"

There was silence for a moment as I recovered from the shock, and then considered the implications of this question. My wife, I knew, having without reservation committed her life to God, would want only to do His will, whatever that might entail. My parents, who wanted only the best for their children, and who saw this in terms of earning the large sums of money which they themselves had been forced to give up, would be very discouraging. My colleagues at the office would consider that I had gone stark raving mad! And me? Well, from quite an early age I had been most emphatic that the last thing I ever wanted to be was a clergyman! Church—yes. Doing good works—yes. Bible—if I had to. But surely not becoming a clergyman! There were limits—even for God!

So then there began three years of arguing with God. He kept saying "Yes". I kept saying "No". I eventually agreed—reluctantly—to go and talk it over with the Bishop. Even more reluctantly, I agreed to go forward to a selection conference, at which I tried to persuade the selectors that I was not the person they were looking for. But all to no avail. They all said they felt that this was what God was calling me to do. I sometimes compare the feelings that I experienced with those of others who were desperately anxious to be accepted by both Bishop and selection conference, yet were turned away, and had great difficulty in coping with their sense of rejection. There was I, just longing to be rejected! It would have solved my dilemma.

After the conference I returned home to my wife and our two tiny children. She quietly reminded me that, on our wedding day, we had given our lives wholly and unconditionally to God, to do with us what He wanted. How dare we now start arguing with Him—especially as His Church was so certain about this 'calling'.

There would be sacrifices—yes, but there would also be rewards—the most important of which would be the knowledge that we were allowing *Him* to control our lives. And had we not said on our wedding day, "whatever that might entail". How could we now start to put conditions on the pledge we had made?

The devil continued to work hard to ensure that we stayed where we were. After all, I had had two recent promotions in the Civil Service. Was I not better off financially now than ever before? And would I not be depriving my family of all these benefits? Surely, I should I be thinking of *them*.

But God seemed to be whispering, "I love them too, you know, and you can trust Me to look after them—and you!"

The day I handed in my resignation, it was as predicted. My parents, who could think only of the difference in income, were displeased. My colleagues, though some of them were secretly admiring what I had done, laughed me to scorn. But something else also happened. It was as though the heavens opened and God smiled on us and said, "Well done! Don't worry because I'll be with you. And I have lots of new things to show you—far more important than the size of your bank balance."

Chapter Three

BACK TO SCHOOL

There must have been a new in-filling of the Holy Spirit that day, because immediately I felt so elated, and so full of joy and power, that at once I felt ready to go.

I certainly *needed* that in-filling because, before long, a great deal of apprehension began to set in. Lichfield was my chosen college. It seemed right in so many respects, but it was also near enough to our home to ensure that I could get back to see my family fairly easily. Yet, this was a *theological* college! What did I know about theology? I knew very little about the Bible. Surely all those who would be starting that same term with me were bound to be well-versed in the Bible and very knowledgeable about Church History, Doctrine and Liturgy. I was going to feel the odd one out. I would never keep it up....

Came the day I was to start college, and I arrived there in good time. I first had an appointment with the Principal, who at that stage was the well-known author and theologian John Fenton but, as I mounted the steps to the front door of the Principal's house, I was suddenly overcome by fear, and wanted to turn round, drive home, and tell everyone that I had made a terrible mistake. But before I had a chance to turn round, the large door, with its big brass knocker, opened, and there stood this huge, grey-haired father figure with a lovely dis-arming smile, who swept me into his study and ordered some tea.

As we talked, I gradually relaxed and was surprised to discover how much he knew about the Civil Service, about national service, about life in a tiny village and about my limited experience of the church, and of God! Looking back, I was able to see how, by asking the right questions, he was able to draw me out, and so discover what kind of a person I was, and whether I really was allowing God to direct my life.

The Principal stood up, indicating that the interview had ended. As he did so, ignoring all my protests about knowing so little about the Bible, he placed an arm on my shoulder saying, "Now, I would like you to go away and write me an essay on why St. Paul wrote to the Galatians. There is a good library just down the corridor—see what you can do." With that, he gently ushered me towards the door. I had only just managed to refrain from asking, "But who was St. Paul?"

I soon made friends—some, admittedly, rather strange. One didn't believe in God! Another did not believe in prayer! But I was reassured and encouraged on meeting quite a few who knew no more about the Bible or theology than I did—and yet, somehow, had felt called to offer themselves for ordination.

Some of the study I found very difficult. After all, I was rather out of practice. But there were so many new and exciting things to discover about God, His Church, His world. And there were interesting people with whom to discuss these things. I learnt a little Greek and Hebrew, and was taught how to study the Biblical texts in these languages. I was to discover the beauty of church music, and even found out how to sing in parts. Social life included a carnival and garden parties on the college lawn, to which we could invite our families. All in all, life at college was very good, particularly as I was able to pay frequent visits home to keep in touch with my family.

It was here at theological college that I learnt the value of having long quiet times alone with God. These were usually in a corner of the vast but beautiful cathedral, early in the morning. In those times I was usually, though not always, aware that God was very close indeed. It was a good time to try out different ways of meditation, and to discover the ones which meant most to me. I still have to remind myself of the need to give absolute priority to the setting aside of such times, no matter what other demands there are on my time.

Then there were three other college experiences which made an immense impact on my life and ministry. First, the opportunity came to attend a course in church music at Addington Palace, Croydon, headquarters of the Royal School of Church Music. Here, I learnt so much about worship, and the different ways of conducting church services.

Then, one day, there was a call for six volunteers, to be sent to prison for a period of ten days, to live as, and be treated as, prisoners. This was intended both to enable us to experience life in a prison and to get alongside the other prisoners—hopefully influencing them for good. Rather apprehensively, I allowed my name to go forward. It was not long before I heard the gates of Stafford Prison clanging behind me, as I was led first to be fitted out with a prison uniform. Then I was taken to my prison cell, with just a hard bed, a table, and a slop bucket in the corner.

It was not a comfortable ten days! It was not an easy ten days—queuing up with my metal tray for meals; being jostled and hustled by the other prisoners; sent out to work in groups sewing mail bags and painting toys. Worst of all, there was 'slopping out' each morning before breakfast.

But it was a time in which I learned a great deal about human nature, about how people end up in prison, what it does to them, and the effect it has on their families. All this was to stand me in good stead when, much later, I was to become a prison chaplain. It is, of course, always important to learn theory, but theory is of little use without practice. The next great project was for the whole college to be despatched to Liverpool, to gain practical experience in the parishes of that great city.

On arrival, we were to assemble on the steps of the Anglican Cathedral, where our hosts would be waiting to welcome us and to take us home to be their guests for the duration of our stay. It was, in fact, to be the beginning of some lasting and meaningful relationships, not only for me but for my family too. I wondered with whom I would be staying, and what they would be like. Waiting for me on the steps of the Cathedral was the gentle, caring, quietly spoken, Leslie Howard, whose wife Bea and daughter Sheila were preparing at home for my arrival. They were determined that my stay would be one to remember!

A delightfully caring, thoughtful and homely family, nothing was too much trouble for them. Hearing of Kathleen's love of classical music, they immediately invited her to a concert at the Royal Philharmonic Hall, with Sir Malcolm Sargeant—a concert which none of us will ever forget. Learning of Jonathan's interest in Liverpool Football Club, there were tickets for Anfield for the men, accommodation for the weekend for the whole family, and sightseeing for all.

We kept in close touch with the Howards until Leslie died, then Bea, but we kept in touch with Sheila and her family—and there will always be a soft spot in our hearts for Liverpool.

I returned to the theological college once again, and the time of ordination drew near. During our final year we were given a list of clergy who would be requiring curates. We were asked to select the one which we considered was right—and then to make contact with him direct. As my eye went down the list, it was drawn to Canon Patrick Shannon in the parish of Kington, Herefordshire. Somehow, I knew that I need look no further. A visit to Kington confirmed this. A curate's house (a lovely old mill-by-the-stream) was to be made available. It was all so unbelievably idyllic, and yet so right. Came the great day itself and, feeling most conspicuous in our clerical collars, about ten becassocked young men wound our way from the Bishop's House, where the pre-ordination retreat had been held, to the Cathedral. I knew that somewhere in that vast congregation would be my family, together with a coach-load of people from the little market town of Kington, where I would serve my curacy. Excitement was mixed with apprehension as I was reminded, first of all, of my earlier determination never to become a clergyman, and then of our wedding day dedication of our lives to God— come what may. At that moment, it all seemed so right and, during the ordination service, there were tears in my eyes as I just thanked God for choosing me for such a very special way of life. As the Bishop laid hands on my head, I simply knew that I was being authorised to preach the Gospel and to heal the sick—but also to care for His people in every possible way. What a challenge! How was I going to meet it?

Chapter Four

A NEW LIFE

After photographs with the Bishop, and a family lunch party at a local hotel, we set off for our new home and new life. They were to be four very happy years at Kington, during which I was to learn so much about so many things. This was certainly putting the theory into practice! Patrick Shannon was a great theologian, a brilliant musician, and a very caring father figure who was concerned not only about me but about my family too. We were very soon involved in the local choral society, operatic society and many other parish activities. It was here that I first learnt the importance of allowing *God* to control the situation. The Vicar had gone away and left me in charge of the parish when, within the first twenty four hours, the phone rang and my worst fears were realised. Someone had died. Would I please go and visit the widow.

I was terrified! What would I say? How was I going to

help and comfort her? I felt so unprepared; so inadequate.

As I walked up the garden path to the little cottage, I prayed that, perhaps, she might be out! But she wasn't! So I sat next to her as she poured out her grief, and the tears rolled down her cheeks. Eventually, as I rose to leave, she just grasped both of my hands and thanked me *so* much for my help. In fact I had hardly said a word!

Later, I was to minister to a young boy who was dying but who, after the laying on of hands, made a remarkable recovery. So did an older lady, to whom I was called— at the hospital, in the middle of the night. What a wonderful introduction to the Church's Ministry of Healing.

They were happy days indeed, but all too soon it was time to move from the cushioned existence of a curate into a parish of my own which, with the prayerful guidance of Patrick Shannon, I did in 1971. I was to take charge of three rural parishes which straddled the Welsh Border—and I felt on top of the world as I moved to face this new challenge. Very quickly, the people flocked around me. Having learned a little about music from the Vicar of Kington, much of whose enthusiasm had rubbed off on me, my first aim was good music, with a good choir. At our church, on the top of the hill at Old Radnor, I was helped by two very competent organists. It was a sparsely populated area but, with a little encouragement, we soon gathered together a number of adults and children, most of whom were good singers who had been waiting for the opportunity to put their talents to good use. With this kind of enthusiasm, it was not difficult to raise funds for new choir robes and books, and soon we developed an excellent choir.

I have to confess that, at this stage, God was gradually pushed into the back seat as, with increasing confidence, I took over the driving myself. Before long it was publicity and popularity that were my priorities, and so I succumbed to the organising of all sorts of gimmicks. For instance, we would climb to the top of the church tower on the morning of Ascension Day, to sing *Hail the Day that sees Him Rise* through loudspeakers—having made quite sure that the media were present!

There were elaborate rogation day processions and pancake races, with the Vicar always in the foreground. On Plough Sunday, some twenty or more farmers would be encouraged to bring their tractors and ploughs to church, and to line them up outside for the "Blessing of the Ploughs". The television cameras were usually there, and there was always plenty of publicity. So these things continued for our stay of thirteen years. It was a happy life, in a lovely situation. Once, when my son (by then a teenager) dared to suggest that all Dad was doing was seeking publicity, I was very annoyed. "No, it's not that at all—I'm doing it for the Church," I replied. I had never questioned my approach until he raised the thought, but my son had actually got it right.

It was during our time at Old Radnor that I happened, by chance, to see a BBC programme about the Focolare Movement, which had been founded by six catholic teenagers in Italy, towards the end of the last war. We heard how, whilst sheltering in underground bunkers from an onslaught of bombing, they had gathered together to read their Bibles. Suddenly, one of them said excitedly, "Look what it says here, 'Love one another as I have loved you.' If we all did that—if everyone did that—there wouldn't *be* any wars. How can we persuade people to take this seriously? How can the whole world be persuaded that this way of life *must* be the way forward?" They quickly concluded that the only way was to start living out that way of life themselves, and so show others that it was not only possible but vital.

Soon, some five hundred people decided this was for them too, deciding to become part of this movement and to live out a life of love. Prayer, ongoing study of the Bible, and meeting together in groups, were an important part of their new life. They then felt called to build a city (in fact it was a large village) near Florence, called Loppiano, where the residents would be entirely committed to living out a life of love. It was this 'city' that Kathleen and I were privileged to visit in the mid 1980s. It exceeded all our expectations. If you want to see what living a life of love really means, visit Loppiano! Everyone was kind, pleasant and helpful and, as they looked at you, their eyes radiated genuine love. Goods on sale were of the highest quality and at a most reasonable price. Everyone could be trusted. There was no need, and no evidence of, suspicion anywhere. Everywhere, shops, houses, streets were spotlessly clean. Everyone was treated with the utmost courtesy and kindness. It was idyllic. We had never experienced anything like it before—or since. A life of love is possible! We saw it at Loppiano!!

But back at Old Radnor I was as busy as ever—filling my life with so much activity that I came quite close to believing I was indispensable.

When I took a closer look at all this, I realised that I was caught in a web of strange paradoxes. While sometimes complaining about there now being too many demands, I felt uneasy when none was made. Whilst I often spoke about the burden of letter writing, an empty mailbox made me sad. Fretting about too many invitations to speak or preach, I nevertheless felt disappointed when none came. While speaking nostalgically about an empty desk, I feared the day when that would be true, hoping deep down that it would never happen.

It is difficult to describe, but underneath all of this lay a yearning for the God I had not yet come to know. I had always been much happier to read *about* God than to enter His presence.

Chapter Five

TOWARDS RENEWAL

Eventually, there came an invitation to go to a new
parish, in Wiltshire—a place we had never heard of,
called Shrewton, which turned out to be a sizeable rural
village with a population of 2500. At first, the reaction
of both my wife and myself was, "Not on your life. Who
wants to go to Wiltshire—certainly not from the Welsh
Borders. But, let's take a day out and go and see it."
When we first saw Shrewton, we did not like it much:
the scenery was so unlike the beautiful surroundings
where we had been. Nevertheless, we walked around
the village, and in and out of the church, spending a
long time in the place. Gradually, we began to feel that
there was enough of *something* there to encourage us
to come back on another occasion; then again—about
three or four times in all. We could not, at first, believe
that this was the right place for us. Yet, each time, there
was something drawing us to Shrewton. The rightness

of it became apparent as time went on. The then Bishop of Salisbury (George Reindorp) became impatient, and he asked me to decide: did I want to move there or not? When I went to see him, he said, "Now listen! I understand you've got horses. There's no provision for horses at parsonages these days. Is this going to be a problem?" There had been stables attached to our previous vicarage, and we knew that that was something we would miss. But Bishop George then gave some clear advice: "Don't say 'yes' until you've sorted out your horses, or you'll never be happy." I could not believe what I was hearing, because I had not thought that bishops cared about such things! His parting instruction was, "Get back and have a word with the churchwardens—and see what they feel."

The churchwardens obviously felt that our move there was right. They promised to contact me within forty-eight hours. When they phoned, they said, "Right at the back of the vicarage there is a lovely big field, which you can have as long as you are Vicar of Shrewton, free of charge, for your horses. A farmer who has a stable nearby has put this at your disposal as well."

One hardly needed more confirmation that the move was right. So we moved to Shrewton—but I must say that I was still the same popularity-seeking, publicity-seeking person that I had been in my previous incumbency. One of the things I realised very quickly, however, was that you cannot do the same things in a new parish that you did elsewhere. I was just beginning to feel my way forward, and starting to work out the details of my new ministry, when one dear lady said, "Why don't you come to Swanwick with us—we're going up to a renewal conference. It will do you a world of good. It seems just right for you."

"No, no, thank you," I said, letting the opportunity go by. But the next year she asked me much earlier in the year, so there were no excuses. In the end, under pressure, I said, "Oh, all right, I'll come." As the time for the conference grew nearer, I began to make excuses again. "Someone else wants the car—I don't think I can come after all." For every excuse I tried to make, a helpful reply came back: "It's all right, we can give you a lift in our car...." I knew then, really, that I had to go, and that I should do so. My next line of defence was, 'I don't want to go, so I'll take a pile of books, sit in a corner and let them get on with their conference.'

So there I was, in the back of someone else's car, a very reluctant passenger indeed. When we reached Swanwick, the first thing I did was to find a place on my own. The astonishing thing was that from the very moment I arrived there, people didn't *leave* me alone! I recognised this afterwards. If I sat down with a book, someone would come and sit by me—somebody who just started off being friendly would end up giving me a very powerful message, from God. The sun was shining, so I would go out to have my coffee on the terrace. Again, someone would approach me, saying, "How are you getting on?" In the end, I actually dropped my book and began talking to some of these people. When one asked, "How are you finding it here?" I replied, "There's a lot of *something* going on here which I don't understand. Maybe it would be a good thing to find out a bit more about it." Back came the reply, "So why don't you ask God to show you?" Then somebody else came over and talked to me. I said, "I have asked God. All I can see is that lots of people here have got something I haven't got. I don't know what it is." Yet another person said, "Why don't you ask God what is stopping you having whatever it is they've got?" To which I replied, "I think it's a waste of time." But, nevertheless, I *did* pray that God would show me whatever it was—and, if it was right for me, that He would give to me what the others had.

The alacrity with which God answered *that* prayer was astonishing! As is usual on these occasions, the conference had a programme with a pattern of worship, a session with the main speaker in the morning and, in the afternoon, optional seminars, which you could take advantage of or not, as you wished. I booked up for seminars. That morning, I became deeply immersed in the Eucharist. I almost wanted to run away from it— there was something so powerful at work that I did not quite know what to do, nor how to handle it. I was in the middle of a row at the centre of the congregation, but had I not been, I think I would have run away. There was so much power there that I did not want to stay— but I had no alternative.

Chapter Six

FROM FREEMASONRY TO FREEDOM

At lunchtime, someone again sat by me and had a very powerful message for me. Then, in the afternoon, I went away for my seminar—one I had chosen, which was very unthreatening. On my way there, I was passing the door of the seminar on Baptism in the Holy Spirit— definitely passing it, as I certainly had no intention of going to that one. At that very moment, someone came alongside me, saying, "I take it you're going to that one, aren't you?"

"Oh, no, not really, I have planned to go to another one." Back came the reply:

"I think I would go in here, if I were you. It will be good for you." This came from somebody who had nothing whatever to do with any of the previous conversations. This was yet another of the many messages which seemed to be coming at me from all directions. So I paused. I was even more reluctant to go into the seminar when I saw who was running it. It was a clergyman whom I thought was a very quiet, gentle little man, someone whom I was sure did not have the kind of power that I had been experiencing from people all around. So, believing it to be a waste of time anyway, I went in. Having already read about Baptism in the Holy Spirit, I felt that I already knew all about it and, sure enough, as the seminar got under way, there seemed to be nothing new. I heard all about Baptism in the Holy Spirit once again. Then, at the end, the leader prayed, as they usually do, that God fill us all with His Spirit. It was during those prayers that a tremendous thing happened.   He had the audacity to pray specifically for people who had been freemasons! I was furious. I had been a freemason for many years, and had always managed to justify it in relation to Christianity. I believed the two were complementary. Although freemasonry did not actually mention or recognise Jesus Christ, it recognised God; so did that omission really matter? When this man prayed for freemasons as though they needed salvation, I was insulted and could hardly wait for the prayers to end, so that I could leap up and dash across to him. "What do you mean praying for freemasons like that?"

He was a lovely man and he took me on one side, saying, "Shall we talk about this?" My goodness, how my eyes were opened by that clergyman, who knew so much about freemasonry, and the inconsistency between it and Christianity. I was amazed and ended up by agreeing to renounce all my masonic vows as soon as possible. When I asked, "How do I do it?" he replied, "Right now, we can pray and you can renounce those masonic vows, but when you get back home, you must take all your masonic regalia and all your masonic books. Build a bonfire and burn them."

"I can't do that, they are worth hundreds of pounds." They had actually been given to me, but they *were* very expensive. The message was quite clear—I needed to get the evil out of my house and burn those things, rather than passing them on to someone else. From the moment that I determined I was going to do that, something wonderful happened, there and then. God must have known that I really meant it. It was as if all doubts and disillusionment were just lifted completely away from me. Suddenly, at that very moment, I experienced a surge of joy. It was almost miraculous. *I was a changed person.* And there was to be further confirmation of this. I was in my room the following afternoon. A man came in who had thought the fire escape by my room was the way through into the corridor. It was as though God Himself were there, in a special way. The man who had lost his way apologised, and was about to leave, but he ended up sitting with me, talking and giving yet another powerful personal message for me. Its content confirmed everything that had already taken place. I was astonished. Nothing like all this had ever happened to me before.

Each person who spoke to me at the conference had been used by God to lead me forward one more step, although I had not realised it at the time. On the last day at Swanwick, the clergyman who had led the seminar which I had attended mentioned what had happened to the Bishop of Pontefract, who was to officiate at the final service. This was to be an extended Eucharist, lasting quite a long time; it included testimonies and several times of prayer. The Bishop came over to me and said, "I've just been hearing about your experience. Would you be willing to share it with the rest of the conference?" My reply was immediate: "No, I don't think so!" So he said, "I'll tell you what. At an appropriate time I will look towards you and say, 'There is someone who may have something to say.' If you don't want to get up and speak, that's quite all right." When the time came, I actually found myself getting up out of my seat (and I am not really the sort of person who would ordinarily do that) and I addressed the conference with such confidence that I could not really believe it was me! It was another wonderful moment. It later became clear that the reason the Bishop had wanted me to speak of my own experience was that he knew there were a number of other freemasons who were present at the conference; and he had wanted the message to get through to them too. They are often some of the hardest people to help understand.

Back home, I built my bonfire to destroy the masonic articles, and *knew* that I was a changed man. My daughter is a committed Christian, who had come to my services on Sunday mornings out of sheer loyalty, but then went off to St. Paul's in Salisbury on Sunday evenings, where she would get some really good preaching and teaching. On my return from Swanwick, she said, "You know, Dad, your preaching has changed. I don't think I need to go to St. Paul's any more!" That was really the greatest affirmation I could hope to receive. It was a turning point in my ministry. It was not all easy and there were lots of ups and downs. But that moment in 1986 was a change of direction.

I have been asked many times about the way freemasonry is incompatible with commitment to Jesus

Christ. I had always regarded the vows a mason takes as being symbolic. But they are horrific, and a vow is nonetheless real. The masonic vows set out what is supposed to happen if the freemason betrays even one secret. If we could disregard the horrific vows, then some of the other ideals such as uprightness, integrity and assisting others within freemasonry would not, in themselves, be bad.

Yet there is another crucial objection to freemasonry, for it sets out to be all-embracing to all religions, so it cannot regard Jesus as the unique, divine Son of God. But the particular uniqueness and divinity of Jesus is the central truth of the Christian Gospel. I had always justified my freemasonry by making the mental reservation that I knew which God I was referring to, even though masonic rites do not refer to Jesus. Furthermore, the horrific vows are taken on what they call the *Volume of Sacred Law*, which is the Bible, and this I now see as an improper use of the Holy Scriptures.

It must also be recognised that some of the origins of freemasonry are pagan.   During my years of membership I had not bothered too much about such 'details'; I had just enjoyed being in masonry for its very happy fellowship. Because I happened to wear a dog collar, I had been made lodge chaplain, and for me that status had had its appeal. Then I had become a Provincial Grand Chaplain—with even better regalia and more importance! These were the things which I had found very rewarding at the time.

I have since been asked about my attitude towards the ceremonies, and the symbolism of 'darkness to light' in some masonic rituals. To this I can only say that we were taught that some things were being kept secret about the higher degrees of membership until it was, in the view of others, the right time to reveal these matters. Actually, I had had no desire to move on to higher degrees myself. One of the difficulties within freemasonry is that there is so much that you are *not* told. I had been encouraged by a friend, also a clergyman, to think that I could join freemasonry with a clear conscience—and I had believed him. Some years previously, I had heard a sermon he gave in which he hinted that masonry was an asset, and he told me more about it afterwards. During my time in freemasonry, I came across many other clergy, and both serving and retired bishops, who were quite happy with what they were doing.

Whether freemasons desire it or not, there is little doubt that more is becoming known about the movement. Books about it have been published, so these days you can find out about their 'secret' ceremonies without much difficulty.

On one of the Christian holidays which Kathleen and I led, a lady suggested that someone who comes out of freemasonry as a result of the kind of profound experience of the Holy Spirit which I have described, should have additional prayer and ministry, with someone appropriate, who had Christian maturity and experience in healing/deliverance ministry, to ensure that all the spiritual ties were broken. This is sound advice, and I would endorse its wisdom for any who have been in this position.

After that profound change, which I experienced at the renewal conference, I at last began to hear God speaking to me through the Bible. During the whole of my thirteen years on the Welsh border, when all I had wanted was to be popular, I had neglected my Bible. For sermon material I went to other books, and that felt good at the time. I had not learnt much about using the Bible at theological college, and had finished my college course feeling quite inadequate. Now I began to preach from the Bible, rather than from other sources of sermon material. It had been quite easy for those thirteen years when I had got away with using other material. But now I use the Bible for teaching—still preparing notes, but not necessarily referring to them as I preach. How I wished I had come to know my Bible years before! Neither had I been taught the devotional use of the Bible—really *expecting* God to speak through the words of Scripture—so this was a new experience, as well. The label 'liberal' would not be an unfair description of my pre-Swanwick approach to the Bible, but after Swanwick I became much more biblically orthodox in my thinking. Doctrine had been just an academic subject at college, but now it was important to me that I believe my Bible, which previously had been just optional reading. The great debate about *The Myth of God Incarnate,* years before all this, had passed me by. It had not been of interest to me, and I had thought it would not really interest my parishioners either. What a mistake that was!

Chapter Seven

CHANGES IN THE PARISH

Now that the Bible was suddenly coming to life for me, as I read it and listened to God more and more through it, the need for repentance and the centrality of the Cross of Christ became the focus of my thinking in a fresh way. When I returned to my parish from that remarkable conference, which had been such a turning-point in my life, I not only found that my preaching had changed, but I also became more confident about introducing new forms of worship. I began a healing service, which members of the congregation found helpful. There were admittedly those on the PCC and in the parish who were not too happy with changes they observed, because it was, basically, a very traditional church which did not want its traditions threatened in any way. Many of them, who felt that way at first, later changed, becoming absolutely at one with me and the way I felt we were being led. The feeling of others could best be described as, "Please leave us alone—we don't mind the odd chorus sometimes, but don't expect us to go further than that!"

We moved as a parish from the 1662 Book of Common Prayer to the modern language *Rite A* service. This was helped by the fact that someone left us £500, which we were able to use for the new books, and by a speaker who came to us from the theological college, talked to the PCC, and persuaded the council to agree to that change. At about the same time, we were given some copies of *Songs and Hymns of Fellowship*, one of the modern Christian song books. Since they were a gift, I argued, they have been paid for and donated—we really do have to use them! This was accepted, and so, gradually, we renewed the worship. It would have been silly and disastrous to change all the music overnight. The encouraging thing was that the organist, then in her seventies (and who died at the age of eighty) accepted the new songs from the new book so well. That was a great help. Inevitably, there was some criticism: "Why can't we have more of the old hymns?" But others commented on what beautiful tunes some of the new songs had, and how good they were as sung prayers. It all began to make sense to people as they noticed how so many of the new songs are addressed to God, and are usually more overtly biblical in content. This led me to *introduce* songs and hymns, and so link the whole of the worship together. It was often hard. Efforts were made to use other instruments, besides the organ, as and when musicians became available. We were particularly blessed by having with us in the parish Bob Pitcher and his family, who had been in the community at Whatcombe House. He literally 'lived by faith'. Bob was a fine musician and his wife was an accomplished liturgical dancer. They spent a year or so with us at Shrewton, helping us forward in all kinds of ways. There were others who came and helped us, including students from the theological college in Salisbury. One of the students did the *Saints in Worship* course with us and that was a tremendous experience. We began to learn a great deal about *worship* as opposed to just singing hymns and songs.

After an experience of the in-filling of the Holy Spirit such as I had experienced, there arises, for a vicar, the question: to what extent is one going to preach and teach about it, and invite others to receive the same blessing? For a while I kept quiet. I avoided facing up to the issue. Then I began to realise that I needed to *do* something. So I began to use some of the lovely songs addressed to the Holy Spirit, followed by a time of quiet within the setting of public worship. This did not always work, because it was difficult to get quietness: when the Sunday School was present, for example. While never using the term 'Baptism in the Holy Spirit', I did get people talking about the renewal which the Holy Spirit brings. The term 'baptism', I thought, might confuse people. It had confused me in the past, which is why I had been so determined to avoid going to that seminar! While not setting up a new house group specifically for renewal, I made sure that existing home groups brought in an openness to the Holy Spirit— included either in the prayers or in discussion times. The term 'born-again' kept coming up—and, as there was no way of avoiding that biblical expression, we discussed it fully and openly. I never missed opportunities, in house meetings and in sermons, to teach about it. I would love to be able to say that, following on from all this, conversions began in large numbers. It was not like that. There were people to whom renewal was happening, in very quiet ways, in ones and twos. They were not people who would have wanted to make a big splash about it, but they made sure that I knew. Then they would just live it out, and this was lovely to see and encouraging to others. The Focolare Movement had already taught me the importance of *living-out* our faith.

At no time did I receive the gift of tongues. There are some who seem to suggest that the Baptism in the Holy Spirit is inevitably accompanied by speaking in tongues, but I am not sure about that. Many Christian friends have prayed with me, that I might receive this gift. I do explain in home groups that, while I do not have the gift of tongues myself, I know there is value in it, and I describe how it can be used. I am open to it, and hope one day to receive it. Some of my congregation had received the gift of tongues and were using it, and so I prayed, "Lord, you have given it to them, why haven't you given it to me?"

There are, of course, issues concerning leadership in a church which is open to renewal—issues which have to be faced. Our PCC at the time was composed of members drawn from the three sections of the church: the 'supportive', the 'unsure', and those who were much less happy with change. There have always been certain conflicts within PCCs with which it can be very difficult to cope. But we had one PCC meeting which was completely without conflict, and that was heavenly! I must say that I long for *all* PCCs, to be truly united. So often there is a tremendous emphasis upon money and how they are going to manage financially—far more than about what God is doing in their parish, or what He would like to do.

Using the familiar image of the local church as a bus with a destination board, there are often some passengers who are telling the driver, "No, no—we want to go that way, not this way." So often the One who planned the route in the first place is forgotten. When once we held a *Listening to God* course it was attended by very few!

Today we are all being encouraged to fully involve our lay people in ministry—but this is not without its problems. It is not that the clergy want to be autocratic (although I *was* brought up in that sort of ministry), but there *are* conflicting ideas, and there is all too often a tendency for everyone to be wanting to go their own way. Often, I contemplated the possibility of an 'eldership' way of sharing leadership. But that would only leave the incumbent with the same problems. There would still be the few powerful and influential lay leaders, to whom others would look for their guidance.

After that Swanwick Conference, a number of other things happened. In the parish, we went on to establish a Mission Committee. Together, we began to explore the spiritual and missionary aspect of where we were going as a church. Because of the conflicts, which proved to be great and difficult, we needed to ask how we could be more loving and tolerant towards each other, before we could even start to move forward. One visiting speaker in particular really inspired and helped us. After a time, though, the Mission Committee seemed to have served its purpose. It began to spend its time with the more mundane aspects, and so stopped progressing. It had been one good and very helpful way of analysing and moving forward at first—but it needed to be re-thought.

In terms of introducing the young people of the church to the work of the Holy Spirit, I made very little headway. I have heard of other churches where the children are actually taught very deep things about ministry in the Spirit, and were ministering to and laying-on-hands with prayer for each other! This is the kind of area where I never had the courage to move forward myself.

I must say, though, that the whole area of visiting and meeting parishioners had been transformed for me. Now, when doing my visiting around the parish, I really knew that I was not going out *on my own*, but with the indwelling, empowering Holy Spirit. In the years of ministry before my renewal in the Holy Spirit, I would consider beforehand, "What is the right thing to say in this situation?" The very concept of *taking God into the situation*, as it were, would not actually have occurred to me before I experienced that personal awakening. I began to experience God's guidance a great deal more when speaking to people in pastoral situations.

Around the time of the Swanwick event, I was Rural Dean. At that time I had wonderful visions of a great light shining out from Shrewton around the Deanery. It was all so encouraging. I felt so different, so filled with the Holy Spirit. The way I was seeing things was transformed. That was my immediate reaction. I arranged for another diocesan incumbent, Michael Christian-Edwards, then Vicar of St. Paul's, Salisbury, to come out and to talk to the Deanery Chapter about Baptism in the Holy Spirit, and I remember thinking at the time, "I wouldn't like to be in his shoes." But he was superb at the clergy chapter. The reaction from the clergy, however, was to listen politely, ask polite questions, and then thank Michael for coming. As a group of clergy, we went no further than that. After this, my view of the deanery cooled and calmed, and I went through periods of disillusionment. For personal fellowship and support, I found a diocesan clergy and wives renewal group a great prop for me—rather than something I was conscious of contributing to. It has been tremendously helpful at times. There was something very special about our times of prayer together in that group, and I would strongly recommend such a gathering to others in ministry.

Chapter Eight

THE GOD OF SURPRISES
OR
"I ONCE WAS IN DARKNESS...."

Shortly after my wonderful Swanwick experience, our great God of surprises came with another great blessing—this time in the form of a miraculous healing. Our daughter, at the age of thirteen, awoke one morning to find that she was unable to see clearly. Everything and everyone around her was blurred, and she needed assistance even to go downstairs. Doctors, hospitals, specialists were unable to diagnose the cause or offer a cure. School was no longer possible, but a three year course at the Royal National College for the Blind and Partially Sighted enabled her, with the aid of Braille, to become an accomplished—though visually handicapped—secretary. But life was not easy. Help from parents and friends was necessary to transport, to read correspondence and other important literature, to check bank statements—and the hundred-and-one other things which normally sighted young people just take for granted. But for the whole of this time she was surrounded by young Christian friends, who prayed constantly that she might be healed.

And then, one day, it happened! A group of young Christian friends were with her, laying-on-hands, and as they prayed *the sight began to return.* Just weeks later she was fully sighted! And we were hardly able to believe it! After thirteen years of this visual handicap, God had healed her. She had no hesitation in telling all those around her Who was responsible.

Amidst our jubilation and excitement, I looked back and could see that it was during the years that our daughter suffered from *her* visual handicap that *my* (spiritual) vision had also been impaired, and that at Swanwick God had healed me, too. We were both enabled to see more clearly. Is it surprising that one of our own favourite choruses now is *I once was in darkness, now my eyes can see?*

Chapter Nine

THE WAY GETS TOUGH.

It was the Venerable Peter Mallett who first encouraged me to organise and lead Christian holidays abroad. Two of these were to Oberammergau and five more to the Holy Land. Not only were these tours an economical way for Kathleen and I to see these countries, and to experience treading where the Master had trod; but we were able to do so alongside Christians of all denominations, who just wanted to be in or near those special places, and to 'feel' something of what it must have been like there all those years before.

There were some very special moments, especially at the Baptism site at the River Jordan, and at Cana in Galilee, where some of the members of our party were physically healed. But perhaps the most memorable aspect was the fact that large groups of people from all denominations were able to travel together and share as Christians, rather than as members of particular churches. These pilgrimages were truly holidays with God.

Then came invitations to lead Christian holidays for MasterSun, which took us to Corfu, Turkey, Italy and Austria. In all of these we were able to share so much with fellow Christians from near and far, and in our travels God was saying quite clearly, "Yes, I did call you to minister in the Church of England, but I want you to see and learn from my children of other traditions too." And learn we did! The Anglican Church, we found, did not have a monopoly of the truth.

It is, of course, easy to thank God for His blessings when things are going well—but what about when they are not? A year or so before our retirement we were to meet with yet another challenge, this time in the form of a dreadful terminal disease—Alzheimer's. Although Kathleen's memory had been of concern to us both for some time, neither of us were prepared for the shock of being told by the GP that it could possibly be Alzheimer's, and that we should have it checked out by hospital scans and consultation with a consultant psychiatrist. Although I had heard a great deal about the disease, I hastened back to my books to read carefully about the short and long term effects, and about what we could expect in terms of quality of life. It made very depressing reading.

This was the girl of my dreams that we were talking about. This was the wife who had not only supported and advised me throughout our ministry, but had been there to share with me the good and the bad times and always, with her quiet confidence, had been able to lift me up when I was down, to encourage and stimulate me. A good wife. A wonderful mother to our children.

An inspiration to those in the parish.

My first reaction was one of disbelief; then of tears and anger, as I started to ask: 'Why should this happen to us?'   I was somehow reminded of Leslie Howard, that dear man who had welcomed me so many years before, as a student, to his home in Liverpool, saying as he lay dying of cancer, "I shall never ask why should this happen to me, but rather why *shouldn't* this happen to me—it happens to so many others. Why am I so special that it shouldn't happen to me?" Leslie was special and I am proud to have known him.

My next impulse was to gather together and read as many books on the disease as I could find and, as I did so, the future looked very bleak indeed. But, once again, it was my dear wife who came up with words not of self-pity, but of encouragement and confidence. "We are still together," she said, "and if I really have got this awful disease, then we will just make the most of what quality of life we still have, and continue to offer back to God as we said we would on our Wedding Day."

Do we tell other people about it, or should we just keep it quiet? That was the next question. But no sooner had we asked it than the answer became very clear. If we did not tell people, it would become fairly obvious as Kathleen's condition deteriorated, and in the meantime there could be some embarrassment when her behaviour was not perhaps as normal as it had been.

Here, again, it was Kathleen who bravely took the initiative. "I have never before written to any of your parish magazines, but now I think I should, while I am still able to do so," she said. Shortly afterwards, the following letter appeared on my desk, addressed to the parish magazine:

Dear Friends,

I always remember hearing about a man who had been to his doctor, and at the end of the examination the doctor saying to him, "I wish I could tell that you had cancer—cancers can often be cured—but I'm afraid that what you have is Alzheimer's Disease, for which there is no known cure."

These words came back to me when, some time later, I too, received the same diagnosis following a number of tests at Southampton General Hospital. "There are", I was told, "one or two rare forms of this disease which do respond to treatment, but unfortunately yours is not one of them." I could not believe what I was hearing. I had always been so fit and well, mentally as well as physically. This surely could not be happening to me.

True, my memory was failing a little—and, yes, I did sometimes get confused—particularly when under pressure. But I knew enough about Alzheimer's Disease to know that there was much more to it than just that—that it was a steady down hill route; that it could only get worse, and that it was terminal.

When I eventually confided in my family, they were shocked—but wonderfully supportive—as have been all our friends and parishioners as the news of my condition became generally known. Part of the object of writing this article whilst I can still be reasonably coherent is to let you know how much your understanding and support means to me.

I do not write in order to gain sympathy, but so that if any of you or your loved ones are unfortunate enough to contract this dreadful disease (and it does happen to younger as well as older people), then you will gain courage from what I have to tell you about my own experience.

After years spent in His service, has God let me down? Well, I can honestly say that my feelings for most of the time are feelings of thankfulness—not for the disease, but for the many *wonderful* things that have happened to me, for my family, for this community, for all the love and support I get back from within the Church, and outside it.

Thankful, too, after the initial shock, for that special feeling of acceptance and peace as I came to terms with the fact that although there was no way back, God's promise that, "I will never leave you nor forsake you" was real, and that already I was safe in His care. Not only that, but in response to the many prayers which have been offered for me, God has enabled me to live a fairly normal life for at least some of the time.

There are days when you will find me forgetful, a little confused, and sometimes a bit repetitive, and for all this I ask your forbearance.

Shopping can sometimes be a problem, and I have been known to forget where we have parked the car, or I had promised to meet Stanley. But, I am still able to enjoy a game of tennis, walks, outings, and holidays, and was recently able to support Stanley as he led a Christian holiday group in Northern Italy.

I am therefore, with God's help, determined to do as much as I can for as long as I can. Retirement, when it comes next year, may not be quite as we had planned it, but there will be blessings—of that I am sure, and I know that the peace of God which means so much to me will not be taken from me.

Beginning the day with God is also very important to me—I am usually in church for morning prayer at 7.30 a.m. It is there, perhaps more than at any other time, that I feel the presence and peace of God which takes me forward into the new day.

Rarely, if ever, have I been tempted to cry out, "Why, God, are you letting this happen to me?" All I know is that there is still some quality of life left for me, and that God wants me to make the most of every second.

Before we were married, Stanley and I came across these words, which meant a great deal to us and still do: "Trust in the Lord with all your heart and lean not on your own understanding; in all your ways acknowledge Him, and He will direct your path."[1] I can only say that this has a greater significance for us now than it has ever done. And more than ever I know these words to be true!

October 1st 1966 was a very special and exciting day for me. It was the day of my husband's Ordination and I remember it well. It was also the day I began to share in his new and exciting ministry. Always, however, I have felt called to support him in quiet and non-public ways and this is the first time in our thirty years of ministry together that I have ever written anything for any of our parish magazines.

I do so now, while I still have the ability, because of Alzheimer's Disease which is something about which there is all too little understanding and is a disease of which many people are understandably afraid. I do not look forward to the inevitable deterioration in my condition, but I do know that when Jesus said, "I will never leave you nor forsake you", that is true for me. And that is what carries me forward.

With my thanks again for your love, support and understanding.

Kathleen

The reaction from the parish was quite amazing. Letters and phone calls of love and support just poured in, and there was also a wonderful feeling of relief as those who had suspected that *something* might be wrong now had the full facts. Everyone knew that it was incurable, and that there would be a gradual deterioration—and they all wanted to help and support.

Help and support was to come from another quarter too. We were introduced to the Alzheimer's Disease Society, and found here not only a wonderfully supportive group of people, but a group who were

[1][Prov. 3:5–6]

prepared to offer practical help in the form of counselling, a day centre, and a sitting service when needed. They also organised coffee mornings and tea afternoons, which were always very happy and enjoyable occasions, and at which Kathleen was always completely relaxed.

But the confusion increased and the logic in what she was saying decreased, so that lively and intelligent conversation was no longer possible, and what I found most difficult to accept was that I was no longer living with the Kathleen I had known and loved for so long. Neither shopping, nor cooking and housework, were any longer possible for her, and there was no word of protest as I quietly took over these tasks. Previously, she would not have dreamt of allowing me to undertake anything like this, which she regarded as hers.

We both needed lots of love and support, but had to recognise that many of our friends, whilst wishing to help, knew very little about any form of dementia—and were afraid of it. Rather like bereavement, they did not know how to handle it. They did not know what to say. And so, whilst they expressed a desire to help ("Do let me know if there is anything I can do"), the offer rarely materialised into anything practical.

But there were two groups of people who did draw alongside. The first was a group of very close friends, who had remained close throughout the progression of the disease, and who recognised and responded to our real needs. They would come and stay for several days at a time, thus enabling me to get away by myself for a much needed day of peace and quiet—days which I would spend either in the New Forest, reading, writing, walking, in prayer or engaging in Bible study. Other times I would go to the Convent of the Holy Spirit at Wroughton, where the nuns were so welcoming, and where there was always a wonderful atmosphere of peace and quiet and prayer. To sit in the Convent Chapel, and gaze up at the statues and the altar, was rather like sitting on the Father's knee and being cuddled and cradled as He revealed more of Himself to me, just a little at a time. (He must have known that I could not take too much at once.) But how I needed those cuddles!

The other group of people who were to mean so much to us were the members of the Mothers' Union, whose genuine concern, love and support, over-rode any fear they may have had of the disease or how to handle it. My mind went back to my days as a curate, when I had received from my outstanding vicar the only piece of bad advice I can remember. "Stanley," he had said, "when you get into a parish of your own, never have anything to do with the Mothers' Union." He never explained why, but I could only conclude that at some time he had a bad experience with a Mothers' Union branch in one of his parishes, and did not want me to suffer in the same way. In my first parish there was no such problem. There was no Mothers' Union branch— nor was there likely to be.

When we moved to the Salisbury diocese, we found that the whole diocese had strong Mothers' Union contingents, and the parish of Shrewton, to which I was going, even had the diocesan Mothers' Union president living there.

Filled with apprehension, I had decided that the proof of the pudding was in the eating—and so why not give it a try! I could always close the branch down later if it became a problem. In any case, to do so would have meant upsetting a great many Mothers' Union members and might perhaps have ruined my chances of a worthwhile ministry among them.

It was undoubtedly the right decision, for those dear ladies not only became good friends and a wonderful support to me in the church, but they themselves exercised a great ministry in prayer and pastoral care, keeping me aware of needs which might well have otherwise escaped me. Now they also went out of their way to care for Kathleen, without embarrassing her in any way.

It would, however, be wrong to pretend that life had become anything but very difficult indeed. It was now generally known in the parish that retirement for us was around the corner, so any new initiatives on my part were not taken too seriously! "Let's go along with it— he won't be here much longer."

I found myself indulging in bouts of negative feelings about all and sundry. There were feelings of hostility towards those in the parish who had never really seen eye to eye with me; feelings of jealousy towards those who were not having to suffer what we were suffering— alongside feelings of regret and guilt towards people with whom I had had strained relationships. And certainly there were feelings of anger towards the Church hierarchy, who seemed neither to understand nor to care overmuch about what we were going through. "Where is the caring church?" I found myself asking. What was it I used to hear about, 'the pastoral care of the clergy'? Was it all something which *sounded* good—but didn't mean very much? Were those who voiced such high ideals just paying lip-service to a situation which they *wished* was true? The occasional duty call, "How are you both?" seemed to lack any real feelings of concern, and I felt was designed to satisfy the caller and his conscience, rather than to assist us in a situation with which we felt unable to cope. Do the hierarchy really *understand* the importance of pastoral care?

Other negative thoughts presented themselves for a while: Where now is God? Haven't I given my life to His service? Now that I need Him—where *is* He? Should I have stayed in the Civil Service, so I would have had my own house to which to retire, and a reasonable pension to go with it; *was* there a God? Had I just been kidding myself all these years?

Such were the black thoughts which for some time just dominated my mind. The fact that I could not go back and live my life again seemed to emphasise what a fool I had been to allow it to be directed in the way it had.

But I then understood clearly that all of this was from the devil, who was making the most of my unfortunate circumstances, in his attempt to defeat me. That he was not allowed to do so was due to God's grace and my very close (lay) Christian friends. They were able to make me see that, though things were difficult, God *was* around, and He would see me through. He would see us both through. And so it was that the terrible blackness gave way to a light, which once again enabled us to see the way forward.

Alzheimer's Disease is implacable. Its progress is relentless, unstoppable. One can only feel utterly helpless as, bit by bit, it takes over the sufferer's brain and has nothing but unpleasant surprises for the carer.

Mercifully, the changes in Kathleen have been slow, but they are nonetheless difficult to accept. When shopping together, it is Kathleen who quite happily pushes the trolley—until we reach the checkout, when she is completely confused about the need to pass everything through the cashier. At home, I need to find new and convincing reasons why it is I who will prepare the meals, take care of the cleaning and do the washing.

Each day now we go for walks, when Kathleen delights in pointing out some birds or flowers that I may not have noticed. These are good times; happy times. But there is very little lucid conversation or real communication.

When our time came to leave Shrewton, we had great difficulty in finding a suitable retirement house or bungalow, but when we eventually did, in the village of Alderbury, we received a very warm welcome from the Mothers' Union there. At once, they took Kathleen under their wing—and, indeed, the welcome to us came from the whole parish—though it was actually a strange feeling to be in a parish in which one was not the vicar!

We love our new home, with its pretty garden and kindly neighbours, and we know that the Lord is with us—as He promised He would be.

I am reminded—and *need* to be reminded—of the words from Isaiah 30:15, "In repentance and rest is your salvation, in quietness and trust is your strength...." As those words descend from my head into my heart, I know that no matter how hard the circumstances, we will be enabled to cope, with the help of Jesus, who always walks with us—who will never leave us or forsake us. To him be glory for ever.

SOME SUGGESTIONS FOR PRAYER

FOR THOSE WE LOVE,
IN TIMES OF DIFFICULTY, HARDSHIP AND PAIN

Dear Heavenly Father, I thank you for your love and kindness; for your creation; for life itself; for all the good times and blessings we have known. I acknowledge that you alone are the source of all love and goodness, and I stand on your revealed Word and promises. Thank you that Jesus has overcome Satan at the Cross. I claim that victory and the power of the blood of Jesus my Saviour, for myself and my loved ones. I bring before you those for whom I care, confident that at the end you will have the victory in your promised kingdom, and that we shall share in that glorious victory, where there will be no more tears and pain, according to your promise.

Lord, guard and protect in their inmost being the one(s) for whom I pray....

Your love for n. is even greater than mine; so, Lord I commit n. to you. Send your Holy Spirit to help me go on believing and relying on you, your Word, your power, your love; in Jesus' name. Amen.

When the going is hard, persevere; keep praying! Keep asking for more of the Holy Spirit. Declare aloud the victory and promises of Jesus, and Word of God: these are the Christian's powerful weapons against spiritual forces of evil which wreak such havoc in this fallen world. Above all, go on praising Jesus, whatever the circumstances.

All effective prayer is based on the offer and promises from God, in the Bible. The sin of the human race has resulted in separation from God, and the evidence for this is all around us and within each of us. God has provided a way back to a wonderful relationship with Himself, to enjoy for all eternity, but He does not force you to accept it. His Son, Jesus, paid the penalty for sin in his death on the Cross. The benefit of that is a free gift, received by faith—which includes believing, repenting, trusting and accepting. In the Gospel of John, we read:

*To all who **received** him, to those who **believed** in his name, he gave the right to become children of God.*

From the earliest times, not everyone accepted Jesus. Many rejected him. Because God the Father raised Jesus from the dead, he lives for ever in heaven. God the Father has committed all judgment to him. He will enter your spirit and dwell in you, if you ask him to do so. It is not necessary to understand everything; but it is necessary to trust him. To receive Jesus as your personal Saviour and Lord, here are some words you can use, speaking directly to him.

Lord Jesus, I am sorry for my sins and repent of them. Thank you for dying on the Cross, in my place, to pay the penalty for all my sin. I accept all that you did for me there, to save me from a lost eternity. I now invite you into my life, to take charge, as my Lord and Saviour.

If you have spoken these words to Jesus, really meaning them, entrusting yourself to him, be assured that you are his, and he is yours, for ever. You are a child of God by His free gift, by adoption, not through your own merits. Jesus now wants you to live abundantly, and to bear good fruit in your life, and for this it is necessary to be filled with the Holy Spirit and to grow in the Word. The Holy Spirit is divine; he always honours Jesus, makes him known, brings new life; opens up the meaning of God's Word to you as you read and hear it. Disobedience in a Christian grieves the Holy Spirit. A Christian needs to be immersed in the Holy Spirit, receiving daily in-filling with the Holy Spirit, empowered and equipped with spiritual gifts from the Holy Spirit, receiving his counsel. So when you have prayed the prayer of commitment above, pray:

Holy Spirit of God, come and fill me, immerse me, baptise me in yourself. Please equip me with the gifts I need to be an effective Christian, in Jesus' Name. Amen.

There are many barriers to a close walk with Jesus. God will never bless disobedience to His Word! Ask the Holy Spirit to show you what barriers or disobedience exist in your life. Doubt, fear and unbelief are common ones. If you have made ungodly vows or declared allegiances, particularly in any movement or organization which does not acknowledge Jesus Christ as Saviour and Lord, this prayer can be used:

Father God, I acknowledge your only Son Jesus Christ, who was born of Mary and who died on the Cross of Calvary, to be the only King of Kings and Lord of Lords. Jesus, I declare my complete allegiance to you, my only Lord and Saviour, who died in my place, to pay the due price for my sins. Under the covering protection of the Blood of Jesus, and in the precious and powerful Name of Jesus, I now revoke for ever all ungodly vows, commitments and words that have held me or bound me. I declare those unbiblical vows, words and commitments to be null and void, and I cut myself off from them. Thank you Jesus for setting me free. Holy Spirit, in Jesus' Name, fill me afresh with your presence and help me to walk in obedience to the Word of God. Amen.

Therefore we do not lose heart. Though outwardly we are wasting away, yet inwardly we are being renewed day by day. For our light and momentary troubles are achieving for us an eternal glory that far outweighs them all. So we fix our eyes not on what is seen, but on what is unseen. For what is seen is temporary, but what is unseen is eternal.

2 Corinthians 4:16–18